That's Like Me!

Stories About Amazing People With Learning Differences

Jill Lauren, M.A.

Foreword by Jerry Pinkney

Star Bright Books

New York

Published in the United States of America by Star Bright Books, Inc.,
30-19 48th Avenue, Long Island City, NY 11101.

The name Star Bright Books and the Star Bright Books logo are registered
trademarks of Star Bright Books, Inc. Please visit www.starbrightbooks.com.
For bulk orders, please email orders@starbrightbooks.com

Designed by Annie Beth Ericsson.

Page 6: Brushes © 2009 Red Fred / Alamy. Page 7: Tiger illustration from *Sam and the Tigers* by Julius Lester, illustrated by Jerry Pinkney copyright © 1996 by Jerry Pinkney; illustration of red hen from *The Little Red Hen* by Jerry Pinkney, copyright © 2006 by Jerry Pinkney. Both illustrations used by permission of Dial Books for Young Readers., a division of Penguin Young Readers Group, A Member of Penguin Group (USA) Inc., 345 Hudson Street, New York, NY 10014. All rights reserved. Page 10: Ann canoeing © Dick Bancroft; Ann on the way to the North Pole © H. Mark Weidman; Ann and Liv © Bancroft Arnesen Explore. Page 11: Ann with team at the North Pole © Jim Gasperini. Page 15: Alina's soccer shot © Tanya Angeli. Page 16: Tremaine's photo of Lutheran Settlement House © 2005 City of Philadelphia Mural Arts Program / Heather Fenton Photo by Jack Ramsdale. All Rights Reserved. Page 21: Finish line photo of Dean © Bobby Cunningham, Gulf Images Photography. Page 24: Veterinary photos © Robert Mescavage Photography. Page 27: Photo of Alvin Ailey © Normand Maxon, photo and logo courtesy of Alvin Ailey Dance Foundation, Inc. Page 27: Martha Graham in American Document, courtesy of Martha Graham Resources. Page 35: All photos of Nico © Leslie Lundgren. Page 37: Jill Pages aerial shots © 2009 Dan Donovan / www.dandonovan.com. Page 37: Jill Pages and family © Scott Raffe /www.raffephoto.com.

We have tried to contact all of the copyright holders of materials used in this book. If we have inadvertently missed anyone, please contact us and we will gladly make amends.

Hardback ISBN-13: 978-1-59572-207-2
Paperback ISBN-13: 978-1-59572-208-9

Printed in Canada 9 8 7 6 5 4 3 2 1

Library of Congress Cataloging-in-Publication Data

Lauren, Jill, 1961-
 That's like me! : stories about amazing people with learning differences / Jill Lauren ; foreword by Jerry Pinkney.
    p. cm.
 ISBN 978-1-59572-207-2 (hardback : alk. paper) -- ISBN 978-1-59572-208-9 (pbk. : alk. paper)
 1. Learning disabled--United States--Biography--Juvenile Literature. I. Title.
 LC4818.5.L39 2009
 371.9092'2--dc22
 [B]
                                 2009028647

With Thanks

This book is dedicated to all those incredible people, like Marva Marell, who never give up on finding the right support for kids with learning disabilities.

Without the assistance of the following people, this book could not have been written: Sharon Abbey, Gale Albahae, John Alexander and Groves Academy, Katie Appel, Chrissy Armstrong, Anne Atwood, Barbara Baldwin, Robert Bender, Tracey Bender, Isabel Bermudez, Mayor Michael Bloomberg, Dana Buchman, Aldo Deodino, Cheryl Deptula, Barbara DeWilde, Marianne Duldner, Janet Eilber, The Eller Family, Joel Emery, Ben Fitzelle, David Flink, Jackie Ford, Jennifer Gasperini, Cory Greenberg, Catherine Gund, Mr. and Mrs. Harris and their son Cameron, Emily Hawkins, Dr. Mark Hayes, Mike Hayes, Chris Herman, Shirley Herrera, The Hrabar Family, Sherra Jarrells, Amy Johnston, Lisa Kalmanash, The Karanu Family, Cynthia Kinney, Rick D. Lavoie, Mark Lawless, Michele Lee, Julie Liepold, Jane Lohmar, Leslie Lundgren, Karen Maas, Marva Marell, Danielle McGarry, Marcia Mishaan, Kathy Mix, Beth Mount, Carolyn Olivier, Willy Pages, Franca Palumbo, Jody Potter, Mitch Porter, Miquel Ramos, Karlie Riess, Bethany Roberge, Pat Roberts, Mimi Roth, Michelle Russell, Rebecca Sanhueza, Lindsey Scales, Sylvan Seidenman, Laura Sheehan, Mary Sullivan, Joe Swaney, Anne Vaughan, Sandy Vazquez, Norma Wallace, Thea Wallace, Tracey Woods.

Photographers who shared their work out of kindess: Tanya Angeli, Bobby Cunningham of Gulf Images Photography, Jim Gasperini, Harold Hinson and Lowe's Motor Speedway, Mark Weidman.

Star Bright Books, an independent publishing company full of heart: Deborah Shine, Publisher and Inspirational Force; Rena D. Grossman, Annie Beth Ericsson, Tina Trent.

Student readers: Cameron Devine, Luke Harmon, Max Hartman, Nicholas Mishaan, Jack Wasserstein.

Readers: Joanne Aventuro, Nancy Carlinsky, Penny Carroll, Elizabeth Craynon, Laura Cunningham-Barrett, Nicole Fisher, Lisa Kalmanash, Kathleen Kinsella, Dee Klein, Lisa Tighe, Claude Wasserstein.

For the gift of a beautiful foreword: Jerry Pinkney, whose life work means that all children can see themselves in books.

For editing support and genius suggestions: Charlie Cohen, best husband; Stacey Lauren, sister extraordinaire; Marian Sassetti, best friend.

My deepest respect and gratitude to those who took the bold move of sharing their personal stories of challenge and triumph: Dean Abbey, Paul Armstrong, Micah Ashe, Ann Bancroft, Emily Bender, Alina Bermudez, Nico Eller, Rosemary Hernandez, Kristin Hrabar, Jessica Lee, Aaron Lemle, Jason Pagan, Jill Pages, Tremaine Peterson, Kevin Wallace, Nikki Wright.

A Letter to Students

I teach children and adults who learn differently. One day, a young student named Margaret wondered if other people also learned differently. I told her about people like Thomas Edison and Leonardo da Vinci who never gave up, even though learning was challenging for them. Margaret asked me to write a book about such people, for kids like her.

Many people have asked me how I met everyone in *That's Like Me!* Well, finding them was actually like going on a treasure hunt. First I had to gather clues to find people who had difficulty in school but still worked hard. I talked to teachers and friends and even people I met at parties. I explained that I was looking to meet people who never gave up in school, and who also had hobbies or interests that made them happy. Eventually, I met Kevin, Alina, Micah, Jill, Nico, Paul, Jessica, Tremaine, Emily, Jason, Kristin, Aaron, Nikki, Dean, and Ann. Meeting each of them meant that I found many treasures throughout the hunt. They all talked so honestly about how school was difficult and how they needed to work hard every day. We also discussed hobbies that made them feel happy when school seemed too stressful. I was even able to spend time watching many of the kids and adults pursue their hobbies. I watched Emily dance in *The Nutcracker*, viewed Tremaine's artwork, saw Jill on the flying trapeze, and met many of Kevin's animal friends. But, no, I didn't walk with Ann to Antarctica or help Jason put out a fire!

When you read this book, you will be on your own treasure hunt. Look for clues that might help you think of ways to face the challenge of school. Think about what Aaron did when spelling tests were difficult, or how Alina learned sounds to help with reading. Read about hobbies that you might like to try one day. Do you like playing sports, creating art or making inventions? As you read, you'll find that some of the people in the book learn or do things like you do, and you might even say, "That's like me!"

At the back of the book you'll find some pages where you can write your own story. If you'd like, you can send it to me at www.jilllauren.com. That way, I can continue my treasure hunt and read about **you**!

Jill Lauren
New York City
2009

A Letter to Parents & Teachers

That's Like Me! is designed to inspire, educate and empower children with learning disabilities. With the help of supportive adults who read the book with them, it can do just that. The people profiled in *That's Like Me!* found the means to face the frustration of school while enjoying hobbies that enhanced self-esteem. Their stories of overcoming obstacles can inspire young readers.

I hope that children will have a "How did he do that?!" or "Wow, she did something amazing!" reaction while reading this book. Such moments open them to discussing how a real-life person, just like them, was able to take a difficult situation and make it better. A wonderful opportunity exists to explore aspects of resiliency within each profile and relate it to your own child's experiences. As you read together, help educate your child about his or her strengths that are similar to those of the people profiled. In addition to recognizing their strengths, children who learn differently must also acquire a firm understanding of their weaknesses so that they can identify what makes learning hard for them. The goal, then, is to help children achieve a greater awareness of their learning profile. Finally, some of your child's connections to the stories may be emotionally based, and reading the profiles may lead to important discussions about feelings related to learning differently.

As children experience success, whether in school or out, they often feel empowered. Combine that feeling with a strong understanding of one's learning style and children are more apt to take action on their own behalf. Indeed, research has shown that when children believe they have the power to shape an outcome, they are more motivated to work towards positive results, as well as to learn from setbacks.[1] It is also true, as many stories in *That's Like Me!* illustrate, that a supportive adult can help enhance a child's sense of him or herself. Everybody can benefit from a cheerleader!

There is no doubt that it takes a mountain of effort to face learning challenges. By exploring these stories together, adults and young people can share the path to success.

Jill Lauren, M.A.
Learning Specialist

1. Mindset: The New Psychology of Success, by Dr. Carol Dweck, Random House.

Bridging My Two Worlds

Foreword by Jerry Pinkney

Jerry in elementary school

Jerry graduating
from high school

I grew up as one of six children in a small house in Philadelphia, Pennsylvania. My most prevalent and vivid recollections of my early years are that of a young boy struggling to balance the two seemingly different worlds I resided in during that impressionable time: home and school. I received full support and encouragement from my family, most especially my mother, and I was not laughed at or teased by the people around me. My mother was a quiet woman who spoke mostly with her eyes, and when there were apparent reasons to be concerned about my apprehension at school, she made me feel better about myself. Because of my mother, I was able to enter that second world, school, the place that made me so very anxious and a little off balance with no understanding as to why.

There was little knowledge of dyslexia in the 1940s and certainly not in the schools I attended. In school, I found myself in the favor of my teachers, yet I was often sent to special classes. I don't think anyone knew what those classes were supposed to accomplish. I have loved to draw as long as I can remember, and I was encouraged by teachers who appreciated and recognized my gift. They were able to see beyond the slow reader I was to someone who wanted to learn and grow.

I was far too young to realize that my two worlds could be bridged. There were two Jerrys: one gifted, smart, and likeable, and the other, a slow reader who was unable to spell. And, oh how much work there was for me just to hold onto ideas as they were presented. I have lived those two lives for most of my life.

Over the years, I have grown to accept that these two seemingly opposing personality traits are really one Jerry. Each supports the other; both come together in a way that I now understand makes me stronger and unique. With uneven grades, but a thirst to learn, I became a model student. Mostly, I tried to show my teachers that this child with so many hurdles in front of him was trying.

My learning disability was not recognized or considered, thereby making it invisible, which caused me to find ways of keeping it unseen. I learned to excel in areas where I was strong and hide those places where there was a challenge. I became very good at hiding it, and I had no way to express just what I was feeling. I supported many assignments with drawing, allowing my gift to shine. I graduated from Hill Elementary School with honors. Making images, making art would become my speaking voice—I drew to learn. I learned to tell my story through pictures, the story of the child I wanted to be.

I hope the profiles in this book will serve as a bridge to inspire every child to be all that he or she can be.

Characters from Jerry's books that overcame obstacles; Jerry working in his studio

Aaron, age 8, and the card he used to learn sounds

Aaron Lemle

Scientist, 9th Grade

In first grade my friends could read easily, but I could not figure out what those letters meant. I memorized *Go, Dog. Go!* so my classmates thought I was reading. My parents and teachers knew I was not. Since I was one of the youngest kids in my class, they decided I should stay back and repeat first grade. Staying back made me feel incredibly insecure.

A lot of people helped me learn to read. My mom made scavenger hunts, and I would have to read to find the next clue. To practice my sounds, my tutor made flash cards. It was especially fun when she rewarded me with a donut.

I became interested in rocks after going to the Herkimer Diamond Quarry [in Middleville, NY] and visiting the Museum of Natural History in New York. I set up cardboard boxes in my room so that I could make my own museum. A friend and I joined the rock club at the Museum and were the youngest members. I gave a presentation about iron slag in front of all the adults. Being in the rock club made me feel smart. It also helped me forget about my problems at school.

By fourth grade, I knew how to read words, not just memorize them. Also, my tutor taught me how to type before the rest of my class. It felt good to be ahead for once. I type all my papers now, and I really like to write.

Left: Aaron, age 7, reading at home with friend, Ben;
Right: Writing a paper

In fifth grade, I got a 56 on a spelling test. I thought it was such a terrible grade. I learned that I didn't like to do poorly, so I needed to study more. I practiced spelling the words all week long. I never got anything below a 90 after that. I still study hard.

I wouldn't be getting such good grades if it weren't for my dyslexia. I had to do so much extra work to learn how to read and write. Now I'm used to working hard.

I'm taking a tenth-grade science class, and I'm only in ninth grade. I'm doing really well in it. I must be pretty smart after all.

Ann on a canoe trip after graduating from high school

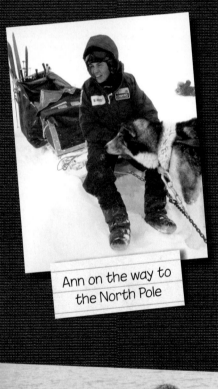

Ann on the way to the North Pole

Students say goodbye to Ann and Liv before an adventure

Ann Bancroft

Explorer / Teacher

In my second-grade class, there was a big picture of the yellow brick road from *The Wizard of Oz*. Every time we got a math problem right, we moved along the road. My friends were marching their way to Oz, but not me. I never made it past the witch's house. Math was difficult for me, and so was the rest of school.

By the time I was twelve, I knew I was LD. I realized I learned best when I could use my eyes, ears, and hands. My science teacher helped me by bringing science to life through experiments. And I helped her by showing her how to ski. I was so happy that I could teach a teacher! It showed me that I had something to offer.

I was great at sports and loved outdoor adventures. I remember looking at pictures in *National Geographic* magazine and thinking, "I want to go on an adventure to the North Pole." So, I started camping outside in my backyard in the winter. My dog was the only one willing to go with me. I told him my feelings about being frustrated in school. He never told my secrets to anyone.

As I got older I spent more time outdoors, going on canoe trips in the Arctic and climbing mountains. In college, I focused on my strengths and decided to be a physical education teacher. It took me six years to graduate because of my LD. I had a hard time memorizing for tests. I took them over and over until I passed.

After I was teaching for a few years, an explorer named Will Steger invited me to travel to the North Pole. I loved this adventure, but it was really challenging. At times I felt like crying, but I thought to myself, "If I could get through school, I can get to the North Pole." Eventually we did make it, and I became the first woman in history to cross the ice to the North Pole. This was big news—so big that my picture was in *National Geographic* magazine!

Right: Ann, far left, at the North Pole with her team

Now with the help of the internet, I take students with me on my adventures. On my last trip, three million kids watched as my partner, Liv, and I traveled across Antarctica.

Even though we struggled, we never gave up. By watching us the students learned that, like me, they could follow their own dreams.

Tremaine Peterson

Artist, 10th Grade

Tremaine in elementary school

In first grade, I used to draw scribble scrabble. I practiced, and then I got better at drawing. Drawing was the only thing I was good at. My friends would ask me to draw things for them because they couldn't draw. They'd ask, "Can you make me a body? Can you draw me a head?" And I'd do it.

In first grade, I had a reading problem. I tried to do the work, but it was hard. I also didn't like to read out loud. My aunt and my teachers tried to help, but I still didn't get it. My friend, Cameron, tried to help, too. He likes to read. He's read hundreds of books.

Because schoolwork was so tough, I really got into my art. I started drawing cartoons. I like black and white drawings. I would get my ideas from TV shows or websites. I like to copy, but I usually change it around.

Teacher, Jackie Ford, helps make math easier

Drawing is never boring for me. It's easy, and it makes me feel free.

Below: Mural in Philadelphia that Tremaine helped create
Right: Tremaine's art; with best friend, Cameron

As I got older, school became harder, including math. In middle school, it felt like I had ten things to do every night for each subject. That's too much homework and too much stress. My aunt asked if I wanted to go to a school called the Academy in Manayunk [in Philadelphia]. The teachers at that school knew how to teach kids who had learning problems like me. I said, "OK."

At first I didn't like my new school, but now I do. It is easier to learn there. My reading is better because I am learning how to sound out words. We've got this Wilson method that helps teach us all the vowels of the English language. I like reading at school now, especially about animals.

Math got better, too. We use blocks, which makes math easier. I am studying long division, and I understand it. I also aced my first science test on the food chain. I read the study guide until I knew it all.

In the summers, my aunt sends me to art camp. I learned to paint, pencil, sketch, and draw there. Last summer I helped create an award-winning mural that is on display in Philadelphia. We also went to a zoo to learn to draw animals. I'm not really good at drawing animals. I'm better at cartoons. That's what I want to focus on.

In school we're learning about the Renaissance. That's a time when there were not a lot of books, so artists told stories through pictures. Maybe I'll tell the story of my life through cartoons. I think I'll probably be famous one day. I want to be. One of my cartoons is already in an art gallery!

Alina Bermudez

Soccer Player, 6th Grade

Alina in kindergarten

Reading with Mom

Alina and her favorite teacher, Ms. K

The first time I played soccer, I was scared because I had no clue what to do. I wasn't so good at it when I started, but after a few practices I got better. I learned lots of moves and tricks. I felt happy and proud of myself. I'm glad I stuck with it because I love soccer.

Learning to play soccer was easy compared to learning how to read. In first grade I went to special classes for extra help. The books we read seemed babyish, and I didn't like being behind my classmates. Reading was so hard that I wanted to give up. But my mom said, "You should keep on trying." So I did.

Reading finally started to get easier by third grade. My teacher, Ms. K, taught me how to sound out words. She taught me the sounds for a, e, i, o, and u. When I started to catch up to my friends I thought, "Yay, I'm almost to where everybody else is."

Although I got better at reading, sometimes I read the words without knowing what they meant. So Ms. K taught me how to understand what I read. First she told me to slow down. Then she taught me to create a picture in my head when I read. If the picture was gone, I really didn't understand the story. I reread it until I did.

Learning how to print letters was also hard, so I traced letters that had dotted lines. My printing is a little sloppy, but when I try, it's neat. After I learned how to print, I had to learn cursive. I didn't really like that. I thought, "Why use cursive when I'm already writing print?" Sometimes I work so hard to write neatly that I forget what I want to say!

Here is my family.

Above: Alina's kindergarten drawing

I work hard in school and play hard in soccer. I play right defense, and there's a lot of pressure on me to stop the ball. It feels good to hear, "Great job, Alina, you saved that ball." When a new player joins our soccer team, I run with my new teammate and help keep her spirits up. I tell her, "You can do this!"

If I feel frustrated in school, I can take it out on the soccer field. If I'm worried about how I did on a test, I can play hard or run faster. But I'm not really stressed too much. I got A's and B's on my last report card. And if something is hard, I'll keep working on it. I know that sooner or later, I'll get better at it.

When something is difficult for me, I'm the type of person who won't give up until I get it right. I might stop for a bit, but I'll try to do it again.

Jason Pagan

New York City Firefighter

When I was little, using words was difficult for me. I was often asked, "Can you repeat what you said?" I stopped speaking at one point. Sometimes kids picked on me because I was quiet.

In school, I went to a smaller class in the resource room. Being in a smaller classroom was better for me, and I got a lot of help. I was happy to be there.

My teachers there inspired me to work hard. One speech teacher played games with me to get me to talk more. When we played Monopoly®, she asked me to explain why I bought a property. She would also remind me when I talked too fast. She corrected me and encouraged me to finish my ideas.

My mom wanted to be certain that I would succeed. She made sure that I did my work and didn't watch television. I knew that if I didn't listen, the chancleta (a Spanish word for flip flops) would be thrown my way like a boomerang. That chancleta would twist and turn and find me no matter where I was.

Jason, age 5

In middle school, there were many math concepts that I couldn't grasp. I had trouble carrying numbers and couldn't understand algebra. When I was in smaller classes, math became easier. My math teacher explained how to do a problem one step at a time. I wouldn't give up until I understood it.

I went to a small college and that was good for me. I still had trouble with math, but when I studied hard, I did okay. I also made sure to pronounce my words carefully so that people could understand me. I am only the third person in my entire family to graduate from college.

Jason in uniform!

When I finished college, I went to the Fire Academy. The classes involved a lot of memorization. I worked hard to pass the exams. Then I was welcomed into the firehouse family where I work.

When I first started as a firefighter, things moved so quickly. Sometimes I felt like I didn't know what I was doing. But the guys in the firehouse helped me to understand that that feeling was normal.

Left: High school graduation with Uncle Fernando and cousin Andrew; Right: Jason with his parents and sister, Tamara

I learned to pace myself and keep the steps of fighting a fire in order. I'm happy that I have accomplished so much. I welcome the challenges still to come.

Right: With NYC Mayor, Michael Bloomberg, at graduation from the Fire Academy

Jessica Lee

Wrestler, 8th Grade

When I was in kindergarten, I had hearing problems. Since I had a hard time hearing the words correctly, I also had trouble saying them. My speech teacher helped me learn to speak better. She also helped me with my spelling.

In first grade, I went to special ed classes for help with reading, writing, and math. My teacher, Ms. Conroy, taught me how to read. I also learned about sounds and syllables. Once we made a rap to help me learn the spelling of a hard word.

When I was in fourth grade, the other kids started to notice that I was leaving class for extra help. Some of them teased me. One boy called me a name. It made me very angry. When other kids said stuff, I ignored them. I wouldn't let them bother me. Soon they stopped teasing me.

Around that time, my teacher handed out forms to the boys for the wrestling team. One boy told me that girls couldn't wrestle, which I wasn't happy about. I wanted to try wrestling. The next day I went to the principal's office and got a permission slip to join the team.

The coach was excited to have me on the team, but none of the boys wanted to be my partner. During my third match, the boy I wrestled was scared of me. I took him down by shooting, which means I grabbed both of his legs. That was the first match I won. I liked wrestling right away.

Now I'm in middle school. I still get extra help, but I don't leave my class anymore. Instead, my special ed teachers come into the classroom. If I don't understand what the regular teacher is saying, I just raise my hand and the special ed teacher comes over. I like getting help right away.

Star wrestler!

Jessica & her sister

History teacher, Mr. Deodino

Jessica loves animals!

My teachers have helped me understand that I learn differently. It's best for me when the teacher doesn't teach too fast and goes step by step.

Sometimes I still have trouble saying words, like names of people I learn about in history. When my teacher, Mr. Deodino, writes a name on the board, I'll say, "What's that word?" He says it, and I repeat it. We both laugh when I say it wrong because it sounds so funny.

I am still going to wrestle in high school. I might even be able to get a scholarship for college because of wrestling. I will also work hard to get good grades because I want to go to college. Maybe I'll be a veterinarian. I love animals, and I'm good at taking care of them. I'll just keep on trying in school. I won't give up.

Dean Abbey

Race Car Driver, 10th Grade

At age seven, I won my first go-cart race by a foot! It was great. I remember wanting to race forever.

That year I also found out I was dyslexic. School was hard, and reading was really frustrating. My teachers didn't really understand my dyslexia, so my parents had to help with school work. I worked hard. My parents would only let me race if I tried my best and got my chores done on our farm.

In fourth and fifth grade, I had to take special classes in the resource building. I wanted to stay in the regular classes with my friends. I thought, "Why can't I just be in the regular class and struggle with my LD?"

When I was fourteen, I began racing Legends cars in the semi-pro division. But I struggled when I started racing these bigger, faster cars. I have learned that when something is hard, like reading, I just have to keep trying. I went on to win lots of Legends races.

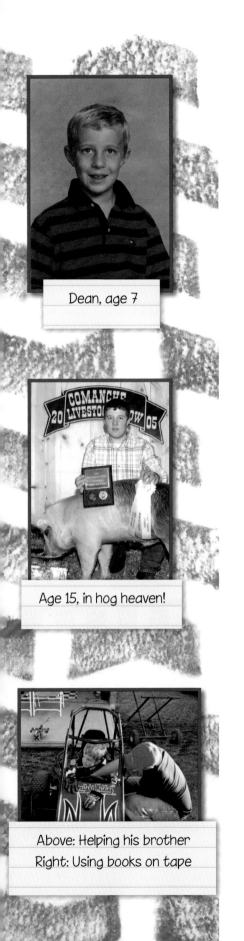

Dean, age 7

Age 15, in hog heaven!

Above: Helping his brother

Right: Using books on tape

Reading may be hard, but I learn well with my hands. Racing cars has actually helped me learn math. The wrenches I use to fix cars come in fraction sizes like 3/4ths and 7/8ths, so my dad helps me learn fractions as we work.

Now I am in high school and in regular classes. Reading has not gotten easier, but I still work hard. If I can't read a word, I skip it and read the rest of the sentence. Then I go back and sound out the word. I also listen to books on tape to help me remember what I read.

Racing helps me get away from some of the down times of being dyslexic. I escape when I race in my car. My Legends car also teaches people about dyslexia. It has the logo for the International Dyslexia Association on it. The more people who understand dyslexia, the better it will be for the younger kids.

I've learned that everybody struggles with different things and that everyone has a talent. I am good at racing cars so I will race for the rest of my life. I hope to make it to Nascar, win the Nextel Cup, and even the Daytona 500!

If it has four wheels and goes over one hundred miles an hour, that's where I want to be.

Nikki Wright

Event Producer

When I was little, learning was easier for my younger sister. She could read better than I could. I knew something wasn't right because everything about school was hard for me. I felt very different.

Luckily, my family was close and really supportive. My mother found me reading tutors. My grandfather taught me math after school. My father explained that I didn't have to finish first to be successful. My sister told me not to compare myself to her because we learned differently. She knew I would do well.

Although school was hard, it was also fun. I loved doing creative things like writing stories. I wrote a Halloween song that my whole class sang. My friends and I put on shows. These activities made me feel proud because I was good at them.

"The witches and goblins are coming out tonight To hide behind a big rock and tickle you with fright."

I wanted to go to the same high school as my sister because I wanted to feel normal. When I got there, it was so frustrating. I could not keep up in math or Spanish. I couldn't figure out why. History and English were my best subjects. They were taught like a story, and I could relate to them.

My friends knew I struggled with my classes. They helped me with homework. But I preferred doing activities outside of class where I excelled. I was on the softball and track teams, and I started dancing. I was even the manager of our school dance company. Putting on performances was great!

Being goofy with sister, Haydn

I received a dance scholarship when I graduated from high school. So instead of going to college, I danced for two years. I danced every day and was taught by professionals. I loved it. Then I decided I wanted to go to college. I enjoyed learning, even with all my problems. Plus, everyone in my family had gone to college. I wanted to go, too.

When I got to Spellman College, my school challenges returned. My mother watched me deal with all of my old frustrations. Then she found a special summer program at Landmark College. The teachers there explained that I had dyslexia, which was why school was hard for me. They taught me how to study. I learned to focus on the most important points, rather than little details.

Above: Talking to Mom

Below: College graduation with Haydn

After that summer, I had the tools I needed to learn. I returned to college and took it by storm! My grades shot up. I was so confident as a student that I even went to graduate school.

After finishing school, I began a career of putting on shows, something I've always been good at. Whether it is movies, music or art events, it's exciting to create something beautiful and big.

Dr. Kevin Wallace

Veterinarian

Kevin, age 4

With Thea at Cornell's vet school graduation

Caring for a red-tailed hawk

When I was a child, I asked my teacher, "How do you hold the letters still?" She thought I was just being a troublemaker and sent me to the corner. So I kept quiet about not being able to read. I didn't know why I couldn't read, and it felt very scary. I tried to follow the words in class, but I just got lost. Instead, I learned to memorize everything the teachers said. I got by in school by repeating words, like a parrot.

As an adult, I kept my reading problem a secret. I didn't want anyone to know I couldn't read because I thought I was stupid. When I was twenty-seven, I saw a lady talking about her own reading problems on TV. The show helped me understand that other people had trouble with reading, too. I got goose bumps just listening to her.

Although I couldn't read, there were other things I liked doing. My wife, Thea, and I love animals, so we cared for orphaned and injured wildlife. We did such a good job that people brought us hawks, deer, and even skunks. In one year, we treated around a thousand animals! Thea and I worked at a factory during the day and cared for the animals at night.

One night, I was "reading" to my daughter. I looked at the pictures and made up stories. She was learning to read, and she said, "Daddy, that isn't what it says. I'll help you with the words." That's when I decided to learn to read. I put words on cards and studied them.

My wife Thea supported me. She thought that I should become a veterinarian because I was so smart about animals. But first I had to go to college. One college professor helped me understand that I had a learning disability. I got extra time for tests. Thea also helped me by typing papers that I would dictate. I grew to accept that I learned differently, and that was OK.

Even though reading was a challenge, I found many ways to learn. I listened carefully in class and created my own special notes. By doing so, I could memorize everything I needed to know. I also tutored some of the students. They read parts of the book to me, and then I would explain it to them. When they read to me, I would learn more, too.

At age 40, I was accepted to Cornell University's veterinary school. Vet school came naturally to me because of my experience with animals. The same study techniques I used in college helped me. At graduation, I was presented with the "Gentle Doctor" Award. That meant so much to me.

People could see that I was committed to being kind and gentle to animals. I am lucky. I have a gift with animals. I can read them better than I can read any book.

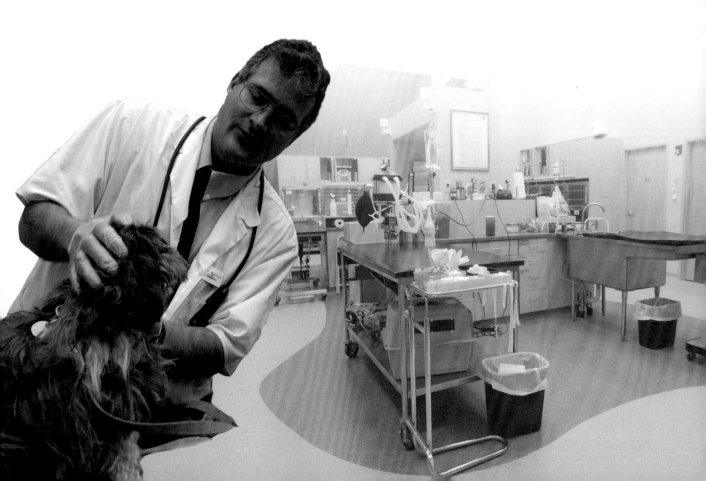

Emily Bender

Dancer, 12th Grade

Emily's first dance photo

Reading about her favorite subject—dance!

When I was three, I went to watch my cousin in her ballet class. I danced in my mom's lap as I watched. The teacher invited me to dance with the girls. She saw that I had talent. So I started taking lessons. When I was four, I tap-danced in my first performance. It was so exciting.

As I got older, my love for dance grew. Lessons were the best part of my week. School, however, was not easy. In second grade my grades weren't good. The teachers told my parents I was lazy. I got my eyes and ears checked, but they were just fine.

Then I was tested for learning disabilities. I found out my IQ was high, but I had trouble reading and writing. I was put in a gifted class and pulled out for extra help. Once I asked my parents, "If I can't read like the other kids, how can I be as smart as them?" They helped me understand that I was smart, but that my mind worked differently. My grandma said she was just like me when she was little. I'm glad she told me that.

School was hard, but I knew I was good at dancing. I danced in *The Nutcracker* with the Miami City Ballet. One of the principal dancers told me, "You always have a smile on your face when you dance." I felt important when the older girls noticed me. I also didn't think about the stress of school when I danced.

Right: Emily dreams of becoming a professional dancer like Alvin Ailey or Martha Graham

I was accepted to the New World School of the Arts [in Miami] for high school. Now I study modern dance and ballet in school every day. Learning from well-known choreographers like Paul Taylor and Peter London has really built my confidence.

I take regular high school courses, too. My LD teacher, Ms. Kinney, helps me with my reading and writing, and I've definitely improved. She taught me phonics and rules, like the final silent 'e'. I'm still a slow reader because of my dyslexia, and I'd rather dance than read. But if it's a book about dancing, I'll read forever and ever.

I am a senior now, and I want dance to be my life. I'd love to go to an arts conservatory like Juilliard where I can focus on dance. My dream is to join a modern company like Martha Graham or Alvin Ailey.

One teacher said I have a passion for dance. Dancing is not just something I do with my body; I also use my soul and my mind. Dancing gives me a warm feeling on the inside. I feel amazing when I dance.

Micah Ash

Micah Ash
Graduate Student

My mom raised five children, and I was the baby. It always seemed as though I was the last in my family to understand anything. I was in a special ed class, and all my brothers were smarter than I was. It was hard for me because I couldn't seem to catch up.

I'm not the strongest writer. In fourth grade, my teacher read our writing out loud. When she read my paper, it made absolutely no sense. Even though it made no sense, she kept on reading. That hurt. The kids looked around like, "Whose paper is that?" That memory really sticks with me because I knew the paper was mine.

In high school, the teachers focused on my athletics since all of my brothers were athletes. I struggled with my classes, but the school just pushed me through because I was good in sports. My grades didn't matter to me. I just cared about basketball and football.

When I got to college, I was lost because I didn't get an education in high school. I took a reading test and got a 19 out of 100 on it. The teachers told me that I might have a learning disability. I asked, "What's a learning disability? Does that mean I'm stupid?" They said, "No, it just means you learn differently." I was tested and found out that I did learn differently. I was relieved when they told me about my disability because I began to understand why I couldn't write or read as well as other kids.

Left: Micah's high school & yearbook photographs

My college had a plan to help me. I got books on tape, note takers, and tutors. I could not believe I could actually get help. There was so much help that all I could do was succeed!

One advisor, Dr. Miller, really supported me. She made sure that I got all the help I needed. My mom also motivated me. She is my angel. I know that I need help to succeed. Because of all the support and my hard work, I became the first of my siblings to graduate from college.

I am in graduate school now, getting my master's degree in history. I have to do a lot of writing. Before I write, I need to deeply understand the subject. I read a lot and take many notes. I like writing about history because I can see the action in my mind, and then it's easier to write.

I really like helping younger kids with LD. I work with little kids in a program called Project Eye to Eye. To see kids succeed is just a great feeling. I also help college kids who are struggling with school. I tell them I have a learning disability, too, and they can succeed, like me, if they work hard. After I graduate, I want a job similar to Dr. Miller's. I want to be able to give kids a chance.

Right: Mentoring James, a young boy from Project Eye to Eye

Kristin Hrabar

Inventor

It's hard to believe, but my third-grade science project changed my life. The project, a tool invention, received national awards. I am known as one of New Jersey's youngest inventors ever. I've even been on TV! So, it might also be hard to believe that starting in first grade, I had no idea what was going on in school.

I used to get pulled out of class so a teacher could help me with reading. I was so far behind everyone else. My friends were reading out loud, but I couldn't do it. It might take them twenty minutes to read a short book. It would take me four days. I started to hate school, and I was only in first grade.

When I was little and everything was hard, I felt like I was saying, "I don't understand" all the time. I started to hide in the back of the class. I wanted to be quiet because I was so unsure. Math was not my strong subject at all. Even today I still use my fingers. If there's no calculator around, I picture my hands and fingers in my mind and count.

Mr. Wagner and Kristin in third grade

Kristin & Dad, first place winners at the 25th Annual Patent Expo

Idea - lighted nut driver

Sometimes when you're using tools you have to reach + use them in dark places. Then you need one hand to hold a flashlight and one for the tool. Instead, what about a tool with the flashlight built in?

My mom and dad spent hours and hours helping me with my homework. Sometimes, my mom would get upset when I was disorganized. I have ADD, and it was hard for me to remember my books or to write everything down. Even though my parents helped me, sometimes I still failed a test. I didn't want them to think I wasn't trying, because I was.

In third grade, I had a great teacher named Mr. Wagner. He understood what I was going through. He always made the extra effort to help. If I got 100 on a spelling test, he'd say, "Great job!" If I got a 20, he'd have me stay after to test me verbally. He knew that sometimes I panicked on tests, so he gave me another chance.

Mr. Wagner wanted us to think of inventions for a science fair project. It was so hard to think of an idea. One night, my dad asked me to hold a flashlight while he fixed our dryer. After a while, I was tired of standing there. I said, "Dad, if your tool had a light in it, you wouldn't need me standing here." We then realized that I had found my invention idea!

My dad and I worked to make a nut driver that had a light built in. We used a penlight, some electrical tape, and a straw from Wendy's®. When it worked, I thought, "Oh, that's so cool. I can't wait to show Mr. Wagner." When he saw it, he said, "Let's show everyone!" Then I won the science fair. I even beat sixth graders! Kids asked me for my autograph.

I received a lot of attention for this project. People kept telling me, "Oh, you're so smart." I also began to feel smart in school because I finally got into a class for kids with learning disabilities. Instead of only learning from books, we used our hands to make ideas come alive. That's how I learn best. Learning became fun for the first time.

My invention gave me the confidence to keep trying, no matter what. I still feel that way today, even as a grown up!

Below: Modern Marvels Invent Now® Challenge reception

Paul Armstrong

Musician

Paul, age 4

Giving Tenzin a piano lesson

Paul and bandmates
from his band, Ochún

In fourth grade, my teacher told my mom that I had a learning disability. I didn't know what those words meant. But I knew they explained why I had to concentrate so hard to read each word in a book.

Fortunately, I had already found something that I really loved: music. I started playing piano when I was three years old. I was really good at it. When it came time for piano recitals, I was definitely comfortable performing for large audiences. I would just walk on stage and start playing my tune.

I took piano lessons and began learning how to play difficult pieces. But my teacher, Mr. Bigelow, couldn't understand why I had so much trouble reading music. It was just as hard as reading words. He figured out that it was better if I could just imitate him. So I did. Then I learned how to create my own songs.

I really liked music, so I stuck with it. Unfortunately, school became even more difficult. My mom had to read all of my homework to me. When I started middle school, she told me I had to do my homework by myself. But I still didn't know how to read.

In high school, I sat in the back of the room so that teachers wouldn't notice me. None of them knew I couldn't read. I learned enough to get by just by listening. But one day, my English teacher asked me to read out loud. I tried to say "No," but she said, "Just read." I couldn't, and everyone in the class was embarrassed for me. My teacher never offered to help. After a while, I slowly figured out how to read on my own by studying the sounds of the words.

School was hard, but I always had my music. I loved it, and I pictured myself playing music professionally. But I didn't know if I could play music for money. After high school, I decided to find out. I wanted to go to college, but I was worried because reading music was still difficult. Instead, I began playing piano at restaurants, and I actually got paid for it!

I wanted to play in a big city with more musical events, so I moved to New York. I met a few musicians and we created a Cuban band called Ochún. I just love Cuban music. Not only do I play the piano in the band, but I am also the musical director. That means I can practice reading and playing the new music before the band plays it. The band performs all over the world. We produced some CDs, too.

I also teach kids how to play the piano. Teaching has given me a tremendous sense of accomplishment. I can do something that really counts—showing kids how to have fun with music.

I'm glad I've been able to take my music to this level, even if reading notes is still hard. I stuck it out, because I love music.

Right: Paul playing at Lincoln Center in NYC

Nico Eller

Eagle Scout, 11th Grade

I was in special ed for reading and math for as long as I can remember. I knew I had some troubles learning, but I was OK with it. The teachers tried to help me, and my friends never teased me. I was pretty well liked.

I first understood that I learned differently when I was in fifth grade. We were supposed to learn the fifty states and their capitals. I could only remember Minnesota, where I live. I'm not even sure I knew the capital. My friends could remember so much more. School was hard, so I spent more time doing other things I was good at.

One thing I liked was Cub Scouts. It was fun when we raced little cars in the Pinewood Derby. In my workroom at home, I made all my cars using nails, screws and a hammer. I still have the cars I made. Working with my hands is always great. I also liked to go camping. Whittling a stick by a fire is something I could do for hours.

In sixth grade, I transferred to a school for students with learning disabilities called Groves Academy [in Minneapolis]. I was still reading a lot slower than my friends, so I was OK with going to a special school. I was shy at first, but then I made new friends.

At Groves, I learned to use a computer to help me with reading and writing. The computer reads books to me. I also use it to dictate my writing. The computer helps me to read books for history class, which I enjoy. I like reading about ancient people.

Above: Nico's scout days
Right: Race cars made by Nico

My best class is woodworking. It's a lot of fun because now I can use power tools. The hardest project was a box I made. I put it together without nails. I made lots of mistakes, but I kept on going. It came out really nice.

Throughout high school, I worked very hard to become an Eagle Scout. To do so, I participated in many activities that showed I was a strong leader. My biggest project was leading a group to plant trees in a really old and important cemetery. Some of the graves are from the Civil War.

I know I have to improve my reading. I want to get better at reading on the Internet because I'll use it more and more. I'll keep trying, even though it's hard. I'm glad I have the computer to help with reading and writing when I'm stuck.

Below: A day at school with Nico

Jill Pages
Trapeze Artist

Above: Young Jill
at circus school

As a little girl, I saw the flying trapeze artists at Circus Circus in Las Vegas. I looked up in awe at the girls in their pretty, sparkly costumes. I thought, "Wouldn't it be wonderful to be like them?" But it was a far-fetched dream, like a star way out in the sky.

In school, I had trouble learning to read. My mom found a learning disability center in town. The teacher told my mom that I was dyslexic. I read and wrote backwards, even my name. The teacher helped me by using blocks and showing me that reading goes from left to right. With the extra help, I learned to read by fourth grade. But school was still really hard, especially history and math.

My teacher also told my mom that I had a hard time focusing and sitting still. She explained to my mom that I needed to move my body. So, I joined the circus school at the YMCA. I loved going because I was really good at it. I had so much energy and no fear.

Then something amazing happened at circus school. My coach decided to let me try the flying trapeze, even though I was really young. He carried me up the ladder and helped me reach out to the fly bar. The first moment of being up in the air was a huge rush of excitement. I loved it. My coach saw I was fearless and let me train in flying trapeze.

— MEDRANO —
JUNE 4 — 21, 2009
GRAND CENTER
ST. LOUIS, MISSOURI

CIRCUS FLORA
CIRCUSFLORA.ORG

CFL   1119745
CFL18JUN09
06/18/2009
BOX I - EVEN
SBEARD

BOX*I

CHECK TICKET THOROUGHLY
FOR CONDITIONS SEE BACK

C   COMP

C   0.00
                         0.00
C   0.00

CIRCUS FLORA
IN GRAND CENTER presents
MEDRANO
GRAND CENTER/PARKING LOT
NEXT TO POWELL SYMPHONY HALL
THU. JUN 18, 2009 7:00P

NO REFUNDS

At circus school, I kept striving to be better because I got so much positive input. That felt great, and my coaches saw that I didn't quit. But by middle school, some teachers didn't understand that learning was hard. My history teacher said, "Why don't you get it?" I was too embarrassed to say, "I read the story three times, and I still don't get it." She told me I spent too much time at circus school and sent me to detention.

I was willing to stay after school when my algebra teacher, Mr. Genung, put his heart into me. He would explain a problem over and over until my little head went "click." Once I clicked, I was loving life. Every single minute that Mr. Genung put into helping me he did with joy and patience.

By the end of high school, I was offered the chance to become a professional in the circus. I took classes to become the best I could at flying trapeze. My coach, Armando Farfan, taught me everything. I thrived off his attention. Whatever he wanted me to do, I was going to show him that I could do it. I wanted to be the best I could be.

My hard work led to a world record. On my 18th birthday, I did a three-and-a-half somersault flip in the air. Then I received an award for being the best female trapeze artist at a circus festival in Monte Carlo. Now my entire family, the Flying Pages, is part of the trapeze act. We perform in circuses all over the world.

I tell kids I meet, "Do what you love in life. Stay focused and hang on with every single finger you can!"

Jill's family is the second generation of the Flying Pages. Her husband, Willy (far right), grew up performing in circuses. Anthony, their son (far left), can do a triple somersault. Mercedes, their daughter (center, next to Jill), is also part of the act. Anthony stands next to his fiancée, Vanya. Eric, a catcher in the act, is in the back.

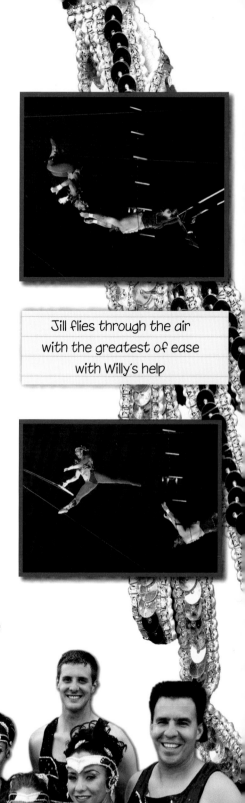

Jill flies through the air with the greatest of ease with Willy's help

All About You!

Write Your Own Success Story

A Picture of You

Your Name   Your Grade

My favorite activity is . . .

My favorite subject is . . .

A Picture of Your
Favorite Hobby

School is hard when . . .

_____

_____

_____

_____

A Picture of You When
You Feel Successful

I learn best when . . .

_____

_____

_____

I feel successful when . . .

_____

_____

_____

In the future, I hope that . . .

_____

_____

_____

Resources for Kids and Adults

Websites for Kids

www.ldonline.org/kids
A young person's interactive guide to learning disabilities.

www.sparktop.org
Kids with learning disabilities can create, play games, and connect with other kids on this site.

www.dyslexiamentor.com/famousdyslexics.php
Find out which famous people have succeeded in spite of their learning differences!

Websites for Adults

www.ldonline.org
This site is a must for any parent whose child has a learning disability. You'll find articles, checklists, references, discussion areas, and more.

www.chadd.org
phone: 301-306-7070
parent2parent@chadd.org
Children and Adults with Attention-Deficit/ Hyperactivity Disorder (CHADD) provides education, advocacy and support for individuals with AD/HD.

www.ncld.org
phone: 212-545-7510
National Center for Learning Disabilities (NCLD) promotes public understanding of learning disabilities, and provides national advocacy for those with learning disabilities. This site offers general information, checklists for behavioral warning signs, and information on legal rights.

Books for Kids

The Survival Guide for Kids with LD* (Learning Differences) By Gary Fisher, Ph.D., and Rhoda Cummings, Ed. D. (Free Spirit Publishing, 1990). This survival guide has helped countless young people labeled "learning disabled"—and the adults who care about them.

Learning to Slow Down and Pay Attention: A Book for Kids About ADHD By Kathleen G. Nadeau, Ph.D., and Ellen B. Dixon, Ph.D. (Magination Press, 2004). Packed with practical tips, know-how, and fun, this friendly workbook for kids has solutions for every situation—at home, at school, and with friends.

Books For Adults

Parenting Children with Learning Disabilities By Jane Utley Adelizzi and Diane B. Goss (Bergin & Garvey Trade, 2001). In a straightforward and empathetic tone, Adelizzi and Goss sensitively offer support to parents of children with learning disabilities who wish to see their children grow to their full potential.

Attention Deficit Disorder: The Unfocused Mind in Children and Adults By Thomas E. Brown, Ph.D. (Yale University Press, 2005). A leading expert in assessment and treatment of ADD/ADHD dispels myths and offers clearly written, science-based, practical information about treatments. Dr. Brown offers compelling examples of the daily life challenges ADD/ADHD presents for children, adolescents, and adults.